See the USA

ORLANDO
FLORIDA

by
Sallie Stephenson

CRESTWOOD HOUSE
New York

LIBRARY OF CONGRESS CATALOGING IN PUBLICATION DATA

Stephenson, Sallie
Orlando, Florida / by Sallie Stephenson : edited by Marion Dane Bauer

p. cm. — (See The USA)
Includes index.
SUMMARY: Highlights the sights of Orlando, Florida, discussing its historical, cultural, and recreational attractions.
1. Orlando Region (Fla.)—Description and travel—Guidebooks—Juvenile literature. 2. Walt Disney World (Fla.)—Guidebooks—Juvenile literature. [1. Orlando (Fla.)—Description—Guides.] I. Bauer, Marion Dane. II. Title. III. Series.
F319.O7S84   1989   917.59'24—dc20   89-32947
ISBN 0-89686-463-4

PHOTO CREDITS

Cover: Third Coast Stock Source: William Bachmann
Third Coast Stock Source: (William Bachmann) 4, 8; (Scott J. Witte) 7, 11; (Todd S. Dacquisto) 9, 13; (Todd V. Phillips) 14; MacDonald Photography) 15, 43; (Buck Miller) 18; (Eric Oxendorf) 37
Sea World: 20, 21, 22, 23
Florida Department of Commerce: (Karen Aldhizer) 25, 26, 27, 29, 31, 34, 35, 39, 41

Edited by Marion Dane Bauer

Macmillan Publishing Company
866 Third Avenue
New York, NY 10022
Collier Macmillan Canada, Inc.

Produced by Carnival Enterprises

Printed in the United States of America

First Edition

10 9 8 7 6 5 4 3 2 1

CONTENTS

Glad You Are Here

Welcome to Florida and its treasure chest of attractions! You are going to have a great time in Central Florida. There are so many things for kids to see and do.

Tourism is Florida's leading industry. More than 40 million tourists come to Florida each year. They come from all over the United States and from other parts of the world.

Walt Disney World is the number one choice of tourists. Each year more than ten million people come to see Mickey and his friends.

But tourists come to the Orlando area for many other reasons as well. Some come to enjoy the broad sandy beaches. Others come to see the **Kennedy Space Center** and the **National Aeronautics and Space Administration (NASA) Launch Complex**, where the newest developments in space technology occur.

Many people believe that, although the state of Florida has a great number of natural resources, its warm climate is its finest asset. Florida has a humid, subtropical climate. The Gulf Stream adds to this warmth.

The summers are hot, but ocean breezes help to make the days nice. The sun shines all year round. The average temperatures in the winter months in central Florida are in the 70s and low 80s.

Beautiful Orlando

Orlando is a prosperous city that first called itself the "City Beautiful." It has added new slogans over the years, like the "Hub of the State" and the "Action Center of Florida."

Before Walt Disney World came to central Florida, one of Orlando's best-known attractions was its many deep-blue, spring-fed lakes. It was initially a quiet, restful community. But during the past five years, it has become one of the fastest growing metropolitan areas in the United States.

Visitors from all over the world come to see Orlando.

Walt Disney World was responsible for giving the economy in the Orlando area a giant boost. The park created construction projects and new jobs. The park brought in tourists who needed motels and restaurants, as well.

Today Orlando is also a shipping center for citrus and vegetable crops. It is a major transportation center for mid-Florida and a service center for the Kennedy Space Center and **Cape Canaveral**. And it is the home of one of the nation's major defense plants—**Martin Marietta's Orlando Aerospace Division**.

Church Street Station

Until the early 1970s, Orlando's **Church Street Station** was little more than a rundown hotel, a few old buildings, and a train station. Today the neighborhood is a whole group of sights and places to visit. It will dazzle your imagination.

The train on the tracks outside Church Street Station is an authentic 19th-century steam engine. You will see real horse-drawn carriages clattering on cobblestones. There is an old mahogany phone booth that was once a confessional in a French monastery.

Rosie O'Grady's is a turn-of-the-century saloon located at the Church Street Station. A live show features a Dixieland band, can-can dancers, tap dancers, and a barbershop quartet.

Would you like to visit a fancy rootin'-tootin' saloon? The walls at **Cheyenne Saloon** are covered with moose racks, steer horns, and buffalo heads. There is also a seven-piece country-western band.

At the **Orlando Science Center**, you will find a large assortment of hands-on science exhibits to enjoy. They include a Foucault pendulum, planetarium, natural history collection, and science demonstations.

Do you know about Tupperware, the plastic containers for storing food? Well, Orlando is the home of the company that made its fortune by selling the containers through parties in homes.

At **Tupperware's International Headquarters**, you can find out the history of Tupperware and see how it is manufactured.

There is a lot to see and do in the city of Orlando—but there is even more just outside the city limits.

Walt Disney World

When most people think of Orlando, they think of Walt Disney World. And when they think of Walt Disney World, they imagine a fabulous castle and dazzling rides to entertain kids.

But that is only part of the picture.

First of all, Walt Disney World stands on 27,400 acres, which is equal to 43 square miles. That is twice the size of Manhattan. Then, there are 2,500 acres of hotels and villa complexes with swimming pools and golf courses.

What is more, Walt Disney World is really made up of three

More than 10 million people come to Walt Disney World to see Mickey Mouse and his friends each year.

Visitors to EPCOT Center get a glimpse into the world of the future.

major parks. The first is **The Magic Kingdom**. The second is **EPCOT Center**. The third is **Disney-MGM Studio Theme Park**.

EPCOT Center is a little over twice the size of the Magic Kingdom. Here you can explore the world of today and of the future.

Disney-MGM Studio Theme Park recreates a movie studio lot where television shows are taped and where visitors can see stunt shows and special effects tricks.

Besides all this, there are thousands of acres of undeveloped land with grassy plains, pine forests, and swamps.

The Park's Beginnings

A successful movie producer named **Walt Disney** opened his first amusement park in 1955. It was located in Anaheim, California, and called Disneyland. Then in 1958, he began thinking of

Disney World's elaborate fairy castle lights up the night sky.

possible places for a second park. He wanted his new park to be different. In 1959 Disney decided to build his new park in central Florida.

He named his park EPCOT, which stands for Experimental Prototype Community of Tomorrow. It would be a City of Tomorrow with new ideas. It would be "a showcase...of the imagination of American free enterprise."

Disney sketched out EPCOT. He decided where the hotels, lakes, campgrounds, and entrances to EPCOT would be. In 1966, however, a week after plans for the "new Disneyland" were publicly announced, Walt Disney died.

His brother, Roy O. Disney, carried out his brother's plans. When the new Disney park opened five years later, Roy Disney named it Walt Disney World in honor of his brother. Disney's EPCOT Center was finally completed in 1982.

The Magic Kingdom

The Magic Kingdom offers 45 major attractions in six different "lands." Some tourists to Walt Disney World rank the Pirates of the Caribbean and Space Mountain rides in the Magic Kingdom with the Great Pyramids and the Eiffel Tower.

Imagine yourself walking arm-in-arm with Mickey Mouse. Directly in front of you, as you stand in Central Plaza, you'll see a passageway through the Cinderella Castle to Fantasyland.

Fantasyland brings to life storybook dreams. You can be part of a Mad Tea Party, where teacups spin around a big teapot. Other favorite rides at Fantasyland are Dumbo the Flying Elephant and a spectacular merry-go-round.

Another very popular attraction in this land is 20,000 Leagues Under the Sea. This is a ride in Captain Nemo's spectacular *Nautilus* submarine to an exciting undersea world full of curious aquatic creatures. The submarine travels into a cavern where you can see lifelike vegetation, fish, divers, and even a giant killer squid.

It is not a long walk from one land to the next. Across a bridge and to the left of Fantasyland is Tomorrowland.

The Magic Kingdom has rides for kids of all ages.

The dizzying Space Mountain is the highlight of Tomorrowland. A roller coaster roars up and down in the dark. "Stars" and "meteors" zoom all around.

You can also see the Space Mountain ride without actually going on it. Just hop aboard the attraction right next door, a milder ride called the People Mover.

Main Street, U.S.A. comes next. A great way to get an overview of the park is to climb on a train at the railroad station. Take a 14-minute, one-and-one-half mile ride around the park.

The train is pulled by a steam engine built in Philadelphia in 1916. It was brought to Disney World from the Yucatan peninsula of Mexico. Early in the 1900s, the train was used to transport sugarcane.

You can also travel along the Nile, through an Amazon rain forest, across an African jungle, and see an angry hippopotamus, roaring lions, and hungry cannibals. All this is at the Jungle Cruise in Adventureland.

At the Swiss Family Robinson Treehouse, you will see how the Robinsons lived on their tropical island. Up a flight of stairs and ramps, a tree becomes an outdoor, walk-through exhibit.

The Pirates of the Caribbean are hidden away in their treasure-filled dungeons waiting for unsuspecting kids to make their way in—so watch out! A mangy dog will roll its eyes at you and a one-eye-patched buccaneer will leer. (You can even see the straggly hair on the pirate's leg.)

Frontierland is filled with old-fashioned "Frontier Fun," which is the theme of this gold rush town.

The most popular attraction here is the Big Thunder Mountain Railroad. It pitches and swerves around hills and into valleys. Then it passes through a coal mine, a gold digger's settlement, and a ghost town.

In Liberty Square, animated, life-size figures of our nation's leaders rise and talk to you in the Hall of Presidents. They look so real you will think you are meeting an actual president.

Then you can go through a haunted mansion where ghosts and goblins make chattering conversation at a dinner party. The walls in the haunted mansion rise. (Or do the floors drop?) These special effects make Liberty Square one of the most imaginative attractions at Disney World.

EPCOT Center

From Disney World, it is an easy hop to EPCOT for a science lesson on technology new and old. You will walk through The Land, World of Motion, The Living Seas, Universe of Energy, Horizons, and take a super Journey into Imaginations.

If you want to see a spectacular 3-D film, don't miss *Captain EO.* It's a musical space adventure starring Michael Jackson.

Also, while you are at EPCOT you will want to visit the World Showcase. You can sample the culture, cuisine, and entertainment of eleven countries: Italy, Germany, Canada, the United Kingdom, France, Morocco, Japan, China, Mexico, the United States, and Norway.

The Universe of Energy is one of EPCOT Center's many attractions.

At this pavilion, tourists can sample the culture, food, and entertainment of China. It is one of eleven countries represented at EPCOT's World Showcase.

EPCOT's monorail speeds safely and easily to every part of the park.

At night EPCOT's grand finale is a laser show along the shores of the World Showcase Lagoon. Laser pictures of dancing images move across the water. Neon lasers streak across the sky, pulsating to musical rhythms. The night lights up with fireworks.

Disney-MGM Studio Theme Park

The newest addition to Disney World is the Disney-MGM Studio Theme Park. This 135-acre park, which opened in May 1989, is filled with action and adventure.

As visitors step through the entrance gate, they find themselves on Hollywood Boulevard. Costumed park attendants greet visitors. Jugglers and street musicians entertain them. Sights and sounds from Hollywood's Golden Age of the 1930s are everywhere.

The park has several major attractions. The first stop on Hollywood Boulevard is the Chinese Theater, which is the entrance to the Great Movie Ride. Here, Dorothy's ruby slippers from *The Wizard of Oz* are on display. Visitors are taken past the Well of Souls discovered by Indiana Jones in *Raiders of the Lost Ark*. Gangsters shoot it out on a city street. And just when visitors think the ride has calmed down, an *Alien* monster appears out of nowhere.

While touring the animation studio, visitors can watch animators at work. Visitors can even see how the movie *Who Framed Roger Rabbit* was put together.

Take a trip to the Monster Sound Show where you can be in charge of the special effects of a scary monster movie. Make a door slam, rustle paper, and break glass using professional sound effect equipment.

If you've always wanted to be on television, head to the Super-Star Television exhibit. Members of the audience are chosen to star in "Gilligan's Island," "I Love Lucy," "General Hopital," and "Cheers." The audience watches the shows on stage and on a huge video screen.

The Indiana Jones Epic Stunt Spectacular is another major attraction. In this huge outdoor theater, actors recreate chase scenes, fights, and explosions.

The beautiful gardens of Walt Disney World

Hop aboard a tram and take a ride through the Backstage Studio Tour for a firsthand look at the back lots of a movie studio. Learn how sea battles are created in the special effects tank. On TV monitors, television and movie stars explain how a TV show is made and how sets are designed. Next is a tour through Catastrophe Canyon where an earthquake rocks the tram and gallons of water break though a dam.

After those attractions, you may want to rest at The Prime Time Cafe. Waitresses, dressed like TV moms of the fifties, treat you just right.

The Disney-MGM Studio Theme Park will excite and entertain you while you learn about the magic of moviemaking.

17

Fort Wilderness

Putting down stakes in a central Florida campground is a great way to learn about the area. **Fort Wilderness** in Walt Disney World offers 827 forested campsites.

This camping area is much more than a great camping spot. It has an old-fashioned swimming hole with raft rides. There are rope swings where you can slide, splash, and swim about in a huge heated pool.

Nearby, in the middle of Bay Lake, is Discovery Island, Disney's own zoological park. More than 60 species of animals and rare birds live here among hundreds of exotic flowers, plants, and trees.

At Fort Wilderness you will be entertained by the "Hoop-Dee-Doo Musical Revue" as well as "Melvin the Moose." You will see Crockett's Tavern, a frontier tavern inspired by the adventures of the legendary pioneer Davy Crockett.

For a relaxing view of Disney World, take a ride on a paddle wheel boat.

Tree House Villa

If you like treehouses, you might want to stay in a **Tree House Villa** right in the central hub of Walt Disney World. These three-bedroom villas are out-of-the-way forest retreats. They are in the heavily wooded area of Walt Disney World. The "treehouse" villas stand on stilts and are built out of cedar.

Beyond Walt Disney World

International Drive

Many people who visit the attractions at Disney World stay in the hotels on International Drive. One popular hotel is the **Peabody Orlando.**

Inside the hotel, the lobby has rich marble floors and fountains. The rooms with the best views face Disney World.

Each morning at 11 A.M. a parade of ducks—real ones—waddle and quack their way out of an elevator. They walk through the lobby, single file, to a fountain, where they spend the day. In the evening the ducks are taken back into the elevator. They return to their special floor in the hotel. The location of their suite is a well-kept secret.

Also on International Drive is **Wet 'n' Wild**, which is Orlando's answer to the beach. Every kind of water fun exists here at this park, from bumper boats to speedboats. A surf pool produces constant four-foot waves.

The park has over 14 different water rides. You can shoot the rapids, crash through waterfalls, and even spiral down a 60-foot water slide.

Elvis Presley Museum and Mystery Fun House

Just off International Drive is the **Elvis Presley Museum**. The museum has more than 400 items that once belonged to the legendary rock star, Elvis Presley.

Just north of the museum is the **Mystery Fun House**. You can play miniature golf with the wizard and meet scary ghouls. You will also be kept busy getting lost in the mirror maze, trying to figure out the topsy-turvy room, walking the magic floor, watching a Whizbang Revue, and climbing through a rolling barrel.

What Lives in the Sea?

South of Peabody Orlando is **Sea World of Florida**. This attraction is the world's largest zoological park. It is also home to

Sea World of Florida is home to many sea creatures.

A colony of penguins enjoys the cool climate of their habitat.

three enormous sea creatures—Shamu, Baby Shamu, and the newest Baby Shamu.

The history of these whales is interesting: In 1985, Baby Shamu was the first killer whale ever to be born and live out of its natural habitat. She swam in a tank filled with five million gallons of salt water and pleased her fans with jumps, twists, squirts, and kisses.

On Friday, November 4, 1988, Baby Shamu's parents, Kandu and Shamu, had a second baby. All shows were suspended so park visitors could witness the "very special event."

Besides these fascinating killer whales at Sea World, you will also see a colony of penguins and other cold weather friends in Penguin Encounter. It is the newest exhibit in the park. You will have a rare treat when you watch Clyde and Seamore in the Sea Lion and Otter Show.

All kinds of sharks lurk in the tanks at Sea World.

If you were scared by the movie *Jaws*, you will also be frightened when you look at the sharks in the shark tank. There you will learn all about the life cycle and habits of these dangerous creatures.

Every evening Sea World puts on a **Polynesian Luau**, a dinner show that features hula dancers, drum music, fire jugglers, and other acts from the islands of the South Pacific. You will hear Tahitian drums and learn about Polynesian history.

Three Strikes and You're Out

Near Sea World is **Boardwalk and Baseball**, which has 30 rides to enjoy. The Hurricane is a mile-long wooden roller coaster ride that reaches a speed of 65 miles per hour.

Daredevil pirates entertain visitors with a water-skiing show.

23

If you have had your fill of riding roller coasters, there are numerous baseball arcade games that line the midway. Or if you want to become directly involved in the game, put on a helmet or mitt. Try out the batting cages and pitching machines. See whether you can bat one out of the ballpark.

There are six playing fields at Boardwalk and Baseball. Two of them have small stadiums where high school, college, minor league, and major league teams work out. From February to April, the Kansas City Royals hold their spring training here.

There is also a baseball museum and a film about the sport's greatest players.

Kissimmee

Just southeast of Boardwalk and Baseball is the resort area of Kissimmee.

If you like state parks, **Lake Kissimmee State Park** is 5,030 acres of land bordered by Lakes Kissimmee, Tiger, and Rosalie. If you are lucky, you will see white-tailed deer, bald eagles, sandhill cranes, and turkeys. The oak hammocks and swamps offer a natural living place for bobcats, the rare Florida panther, and other wildlife.

This park is a piece of living history. It is the site of an 1876 cow camp, where one of the few remaining herds of scrub cattle still roams. "Scrub cows" were descended from the same ancestor as the Texas longhorns—Spanish cattle from Andalusia. When they were first brought to Florida in the 1820s, they were not much bigger than donkeys.

As you walk down the trail to the camp, you can see a cow hunter at work in a frontier cow camp. Every spring the cows are rounded up and branded. In the 1800s, the Kissimmee region was the heart of south Florida's frontier cattle country. Look for the holding pen. It is similar to the pens built along the cattle drive to

Punta Rassa (on the West Coast). From there, the cows were loaded aboard ships and sent to Cuba. The cattlemen were paid in gold Spanish doubloons, the common currency of the south Florida frontier.

Lake Kissimmee State Park offers picnicking, fishing, boating, and nature study. Swimming, however, is not permitted.

Rodeos and Bluegrass Music

Every Saturday evening there is a rodeo at **River Ranch Resort** in Kissimmee. You can watch working cowboys try to stay aboard 2,000-pound bulls or bareback broncos.

In addition, the 750-acre ranch offers hayrides and horseback trail rides for those 12 years and older. The trails wind through large oaks hung with Spanish moss, towering pines, palms, and

A cowboy tries to stay on top of a bronco at one of the weekly rodeos held in central Florida.

palmettos (short palms). You can hear cowboys singing and visit a saloon like those of the Wild West. Belly up to the bar and order a sarsaparilla, a drink similar to root beer.

If you are at the River Ranch Resort on the 4th of July, you can enjoy a craft show, family activities, and a fireworks display.

The Kissimmee Valley Livestock Market holds public auctions in the state. More than 100 head of cattle change hands each hour. Florida is the top producer of beef cattle east of the Mississippi.

The second weekend in March the Bluegrass Festival takes place in Kissimmee.

Have you ever heard a bluegrass band? Now is your chance. Performers and fans gather together in the Silver Spurs Arena for three days of fun-packed guitar playing and singing.

Gatorland Zoo

How would you like to sample bite-sized morsels of alligator meat? Would you like to take a can of alligator chowder back to your friends?

More than 4,000 alligators make their home at Gatorland Zoo.

Ever since 1949, visitors to central Florida have been visiting the 4,800 alligators at **Gatorland Zoo** near Kissimmee.

Some of these green "swamp dragons" are as long as 15 feet. They can weigh more than 1,000 pounds. Due to a special controlled-growth program, some of the zoo's alligators are the largest in the world.

There's a daily "Gator Jumparoo" show where trained alligators leap high out of the water for food.

Places of the Past and Future

Sometimes it is hard to imagine how life was in past centuries. But you can get a glimpse of the days of knights, castles, and legends when you visit **Medieval Times**.

In a modern medieval manor house, you'll enjoy a four-course medieval feast while you cheer your favorite knight on to victory. The knights compete on horseback in medieval tournament games, jousting matches, and sword-to-sword combat.

At the end of the tournament, a knight who has won may be-

Knights joust for trophies while visitors cheer them on.

stow a flower or other gift upon a young guest...making it a night to remember.

Just down the road from Medieval Times is **Xanadu**.

Enter a time warp and look into the future of home construction in the 21st century. There is an indoor pool, a waterfall-spa in the master bedroom, a solar sauna, a greenhouse, and all kinds of new electronic gadgetry.

Before you leave the resort area of Kissimmee you should plan to visit **Water Mania**. This is Kissimmee's new water park. Water Mania features Florida's largest "wave" pool. There are eight exciting new slides for kids to enjoy, also.

St. Augustine

City Named After a Saint

About 100 miles north of Orlando is the city of **St. Augustine**. Much of Florida's history began in this city.

In late March 1513, **Ponce de León** landed on Florida's northeastern coast near St. Augustine. He saw blooming azaleas, magnolias, and other flowering plants. Ponce de León called it "Pascua Florida," which in Spanish means "Feast of Flowers." Later this name was shortened to Florida. He claimed it for the Spanish king.

A permanent colony was founded on this spot by **Captain General Pedro Menéndez de Avilés** on August 28, 1565. This day became known as St. Augustine's Day. He named the new colony St. Augustine after an early Christian saint. The city of St. Augustine is rich in history. It is our country's oldest settlement.

Every August there is a three-day "Days in Spain Festival" in St. Augustine in which the whole city celebrates its founding. If you are there visiting, you will see a grand fireworks display, parades, and nightly entertainment. There is everything from sword fighting to a Spanish beard contest, music, dancing, and Spanish food.

St. Augustine, Florida, is the oldest settlement in the United States.

A traditional Easter Parade called Parada de los Caballos y Coches (Parade of Horses and Coaches) marches through the city. Beautiful horses are decked out in Easter bonnets donated by famous women.

The Easter festivities include a drill team, color guard, beauty queens, and the Easter Festival Royal Family with its entourage of 100 costumed attendants.

San Augustin Antiguo

Back in the 1600s, St. Augustine was a settlement of about 700 people. There was a hospital, a church, a market, and a gristmill (a mill for grinding grain into flour). A large fort stood near the harbor where the soldiers lived. Small farms stood just outside of town.

Today **San Augustin Antiguo** is St. Augustine's main preservation area. It is a Spanish colonial village with homes much like the ones of the 1600s. There is a section of the village where you can see how the people worked then. It includes demonstrations by a blacksmith, leather worker, potter, silversmith, printer, baker, and woodturner.

There is also an old schoolhouse with students seated at their wooden desks and a schoolmaster leading them in their studies.

On the same street is the **Museum of Yesterday's Toys**. The toys are inside an old rustic home.

Castillo de San Marcos is the city's giant landmark. It is a stone fort. The fort is made out of coquina (pronounced "koh-keen-a"), a soft yellow stone formed from solidified masses of sand and shells. The coquina, which means cockle shell in Spanish, was quarried from deposits on nearby Anastasia Island. It was hauled by oxcart and floated on barges across the inlet.

The fort dates back to the early 1670s. Queen Mariana, ruler for her young son King Carlos II, ordered the walled fortress built to protect the Spanish settlement of St. Augustine from pirate attacks.

To carry out these orders, a new governor was sent to Florida.

St. Augustine's Castillo de San Marcos is a huge stone fort. Built in the 1670s, it has withstood many attacks.

Don Manuel de Cendaya arrived in St. Augustine in July 1671. Within a month, work on the fort was begun.

Skilled workers came from Cuba to help build the fort. Native Americans, Spaniards, convicts, and African slaves also worked on it.

Construction was not completed until August 1695. It was over 20 years after Cendaya started the project. The fort stands 35 feet high in most places. The walls are more than 10 feet thick. There are lookout towers, wall openings for cannons, quarters for soldiers, a parade ground, and a courtyard. The fort is surrounded by a moat. The space inside the fort can hold as many as 1,500 people.

Queen Anne's War

The first test of the new fort's strength came in 1702. Castillo de San Marcos was attacked in the early part of Queen Anne's War. In this war, the English were the enemy of the Spanish people in the fort.

The governor of Carolina, James Moore, sent an army of English soldiers to attack St. Augustine. He wanted to make Florida an English colony. If he had succeeded, England would have controlled the entire eastern coast of North America.

Governor Moore placed Robert Daniel in charge of an English army. Daniel marched the army to the Spanish colony of St. Augustine. He expected to do battle. However, when he got there the city was empty. Florida's governor, Joseph de Zuniga, had received reports that the English army was on its way. He had ordered the people of St. Augustine inside the fort.

When Governor Moore arrived later with a large navy, he attacked Castillo de San Marcos with cannons. He did this for more than a month. But the cannons could not penetrate the fort's thick walls. Finally, Moore burned the city of St. Augustine to the ground and went back to Carolina.

In an effort to prevent another invasion, the Spanish built embankments and thick fences of stakes on its exposed sides. This defense made St. Augustine a well-protected walled city.

In 1821 Spain gave up Florida to the United States. The fort was renamed the Castillo Fort Marion. It was used as a fort and prison until 1900.

Over the years many groups lived in the fort: American Revolutionaries, Seminole Indians, Confederate and Union troops, and American deserters from the Spanish-American War.

In 1924 the fort was declared a national monument. Today, the National Park Service gives tours, talks, and exhibits on the history of the fort and Spanish Florida. There are firing demonstrations of antique weapons several times a day.

The **Gun Shop and Museum of Weapons** at St. Augustine has a collection of Civil War guns, swords, pistols, and muskets.

St. Augustine Sightseeing

Many tourists who visit St. Augustine like to visit the **Fountain of Youth**. They want to drink from the same waters that, supposedly, Ponce de León was searching for. De León believed this water could make him stay young forever.

You can also see a memorial to Ponce de León, a planetarium, a museum, and a swan pool.

If you like castles, visit **Zorayda Castle**. The castle is a copy of a Spanish *Alhambra* (palace) complete with harem quarters. (The women of the household lived in the harem.) There is also an art collection.

The **St. Augustine Alligator Farm** has many huge alligators. Other Florida wildlife may be seen along a nature walk through a swamp.

In 1893, when the alligator farm was built, empire-builder Henry Flagler extended the railroad he was building in central Florida to St. Augustine.

Soon life in the city began to center around the wonderful resorts he built—the Ponce de León and Alcazar hotels.

Visitors from up north came from the cold northern climates by steamer and train to spend the winter. They spent it in high style, dancing under the stars on top of the old fort and parading in carriages down Avenida Menéndez alongside the bay.

Flagler's Alcazar Hotel closed in the 1930s during the Great Depression. The hotel stayed empty until Chicago millionaire Otto C. Lightner bought it. He made it into the **Lightner Museum**.

Lightner Museum became the South's largest exhibit of antiques, mechanical musical instruments, and other relics. There are three floors to the museum.

You will see a 17-shop Victorian Village, Tiffany glass, Napoleon's desk, and a quilt made by Abraham Lincoln's wife.

Flagler's other resort, the Ponce de León, became Flagler College.

St. Augustine Sightseeing Trains are a great way to see the city. The ride is a seven-mile tour of all the places you can visit.

Visitors can tour the track at the Daytona International Speedway when no major races are scheduled.

Daytona Beach

If you look on a map, you will see **Daytona Beach** between St. Augustine and Orlando. It is on Florida's eastern coast.

Daytona calls itself the "World's Most Famous Beach." For years and years, tourists have come to Daytona Beach to sun, sleep, play, and drive on the well packed sand.

The **Ocean Pier** at Main Street on the Atlantic Ocean in Daytona Beach offers fishing and swimming. And you can see the ocean and surrounding area from the 100-foot-tall **Space Needle.**

Where the Cars Are

Today, the Daytona Beach speed limit is 10 miles per hour (mph). But that wasn't always so. Before the **Daytona Interna-**

The sand of Daytona Beach, Florida, is so well packed that cars can drive on it.

tional Speedway was constructed in 1959, cars went as fast as 276 mph on the beach.

In 1928, Captain Malcolm Campbell, a millionaire English sportsman, brought a car powered by an aircraft engine to Daytona Beach. First he took his car to a record of 206.96 mph, in later years to 246 mph, then 253 mph, 272 mph, and finally 276 mph.

Each year in February, the Daytona International Speedway is packed with race followers who come here for two "speed weeks." In July the Firecracker 400 and the Paul Revere 250 are major events on racing calendars. The International Motor Sports Association (ISMA) National Championship takes place in November.

When no major race events are scheduled, you can take a tour of the track. All-time greats like Richard Petty, A.J. Foyt, Mario Andretti, Bobby Allison, and Fireball Roberts have raced here. You will see Pit Road and Victory Lane and the garage area where the mechanics work on the cars.

The grandstands seat more than 85,000. The infield holds between 40,000 and 50,000 persons. It is a grassy area where recreational vehicles can park overnight. The people sit up on their roofs to see the race. To get to the infield, you have to go through a tunnel under the race track.

Journey into Space

In 1968 the first flight around the moon was launched from the new Kennedy Space Center, located near Daytona Beach. The next year, the first voyage to the moon began from this site. Flights continue to be launched from these pads.

At the Kennedy Space Center and NASA Launch Complex, which are now called **Spaceport USA**, you will want to stop first at the visitor center on Merritt Island. The visitor center is between the mainland and the Cape. It is about six miles south of Titusville, Florida.

Here, there are huge rockets and spacecraft. Inside the center you will see an authentic piece of moon rock and get a close look

Rockets, Apollo capsules, and a piece of moon rock can be seen at Spaceport USA.

at Apollo capsules, rocket engines, and a lunar module.

In the Hall of History, you will find out more about the space program.

A two-hour NASA bus tour leaves every few minutes from the visitor center of the Kennedy Space Center. Another tour of the Cape Canaveral facilities is conducted only at certain times.

On your tour of the Space Center, you will be able to walk around the huge Saturn V/Apollo space vehicle that sent astronauts to the moon.

You will pass the 52-story Vehicle Assembly Building. Look for the transporters that carry spacecraft to the launching pads and, of course, the launch pads. You can see the huge Mobile Launcher platforms, on which space shuttles are assembled. And you will see the powerful Crawler/Transporter that hauls the platform and shuttle to the pad.

The tour of Cape Canaveral includes a visit to the **Mercury Mission Control Center** and the **Air Force Missiles and Space Museum.** The museum houses early space vehicles and launch pads that made Cape Canaveral a well-known name throughout the world. Among them are the pad and gantry (platform) where America's first satellite was launched into orbit in 1958.

The IMAX Theatre at Kennedy Space Center presents the film *The Dream is Alive.* It includes actual footage shot by NASA astronauts in space. It shows the launch and landing of the Space Shuttle Columbia. You can almost feel the floor tremble as you watch the space shuttle lift off on the giant five-and-one-half-story screen.

There is another free theater at the west end of Spaceport Central—the primary exhibition building. Space movies and slide presentations are shown there regularly throughout the day.

Town of Surprises

The pleasant community of **Lake Wales, Florida**, is 250 feet above sea level. This is the highest elevation of any city in peninsular Florida. It is about 48 miles south of Orlando.

Bok Tower Gardens, one of Florida's most famous landmarks, is located at Lake Wales.

The historic bell tower at the center of the gardens houses one of the world's great carillons. The carillon is made up of 53 bronze bells that range in weight from 17 pounds to 12 tons.

When the bell ringer strikes the wooden keys, either with the base of a closed fist or with a foot, the corresponding bells ring.

The tower is constructed of pink and gray Georgia marble and Florida coquina stone. There are seven working levels in the tower, including the first carillon library in the United States and the bell ringer's study. At the top of the tower on the outside are sculptures of stone herons.

The Bok Tower Gardens were designed in 1928 by **Frederick Law Olmsted, Jr.,** son of the famous planner of New York's Central Park. The park was dedicated by President Calvin Coolidge in

1929 to the American people on behalf of Edward Bok. Bok was an immigrant from the Netherlands who became a successful New York writer and editor.

The gardens are home to a colony of wood ducks and 126 other wild bird species. You can follow shady paths that wind through forests of lush green ferns, palms, and oaks.

Thousands of visitors come every spring to Lake Wales to see the annual Black Hills Passion Play. This is a drama of the last week of Jesus' life on earth.

Professional actors play the major parts in the play. Local residents and visitors sometimes fill in as extras in scenes requiring crowds.

If you like museums, and railroad memorabilia in particular, you will enjoy Lake Wales's museum and cultural center.

The railroad at Lake Wales played an important role in the early

Bok Tower in Lake Wales, Florida, houses 53 bronze bells.

development of this area. Its local people felt it was appropriate that the museum be located in a former Atlantic Coast Line railway depot built in 1928. This was the first building built in Lake Wales.

Photographs, newspapers, and exhibits of early industries, like turpentine, cattle ranching, and citrus farming, tell the region's history. There is also an authentic turn-of-the-century railway car sitting outside on the tracks.

Right in the heart of Lake Wales is a popular attraction, and it is free!

Just ask for directions to **Spook Hill.** When you see the road, you will notice it goes up a steep hill.

As visitors drive up the hill, they do not notice anything out of the ordinary. But as soon as the driver takes the car out of gear, something unusual happens.

Mysteriously, the car begins to move slowly—uphill!

Cities and Towns Around Orlando

Sanford and Blue Spring

Central Florida Zoo in Sanford, Florida, is the home of more than 400 wild and exotic animals. You will see alligators, crocodiles, lions, tigers, snakes, elephants, parrots, and baboons. There are also pony rides, animal-feeding demonstrations, and a nature trail winding through a swamp.

Thousands of visitors to central Florida come to see the manatees who live in the waters of **Blue Spring, Florida**. Sadly, many of these gentle mammals have been injured, and even killed, by boat propellers.

Manatees are about 10 feet long, nearly black, and almost with-

The manatees of Blue Spring, Florida, remind many people of the mermaids of myth.

out hair. You can see the manatees at Blue Spring from mid-November to the end of March when the weather is cool.

They gather each winter in Blue Spring Run, where the year-round 72-degree temperature offers a refuge from the colder water of the St. Johns River.

Winter Park

Winter Park, Florida, is a suburb of Orlando settled by New Englanders in the 1800s.

Mead Botanical Gardens is a 55-acre park at the southern part of town. There are gardens, greenhouses, and trails through a chain of lakes and canals.

On Genius Drive in Winter Park, along a winding sand road that leads to lush plants and mansions, you will see peacocks.

The 150-acre preservation area where these birds live belonged to a wealthy family whose name was Genius. It is now owned by the Winter Park Land Company and is open to the public on Sundays from noon to 6 P.M.

Sometimes visitors are lucky enough to see a proud male spread his colorful fantail during the courtship ritual. Visitors may feed the peacocks peanuts or sunflower seeds.

Longwood

The **Inside-Outside House** in **Longwood** has an odd architectural design. The building framework of studs and wooden plates are visible on the outside. In most houses, you find the framework on the inside.

The house was first taken apart and moved from Boston by ship down the Atlantic Ocean to Jacksonville, Florida, in 1873. From there it went by river barge to Sanford and then 20 miles farther by mule cart to Altamonte Springs, where it was put back together. The Inside-Outside House moved once more from Altamonte Springs to its permanent home in Longwood.

You will go many places and see many sights before you leave

Exhibits like Spaceship Earth at EPCOT Center may make you feel as if Florida is an exotic new world.

Orlando, Florida—from the Inside-Outside House to the carillons at Bok Tower Gardens to Walt Disney World—and you'll certainly enjoy them all!

Orlando Statistics

City nicknames: The City Beautiful

The Hub of the State

The Action Center of Florida

Incorporated as a town: 1875

Warmest month: August, average temperature is 81 degrees Fahrenheit

Coldest month: January, average temperature is 61 degrees Fahrenheit

Number of lakes in the city limits: 54

Number of parks in the city limits: 47

Number of hotel rooms in the Orlando area (as of 1988): 58,000

Number of visitors to the Magic Kingdom and EPCOT Center in 1987: 23 million

For More Information

For more information about Orlando and its many activities, write to:

Walt Disney World Company
P.O. Box 10,040
Lake Buena Vista, FL 32830-0040

Lake Kissimmee State Park
14248 Camp Mack Road
Lake Wales, FL 33853

Orlando Area Chamber of Commerce
P.O. Box 1913
Orlando, FL 32802

City Map

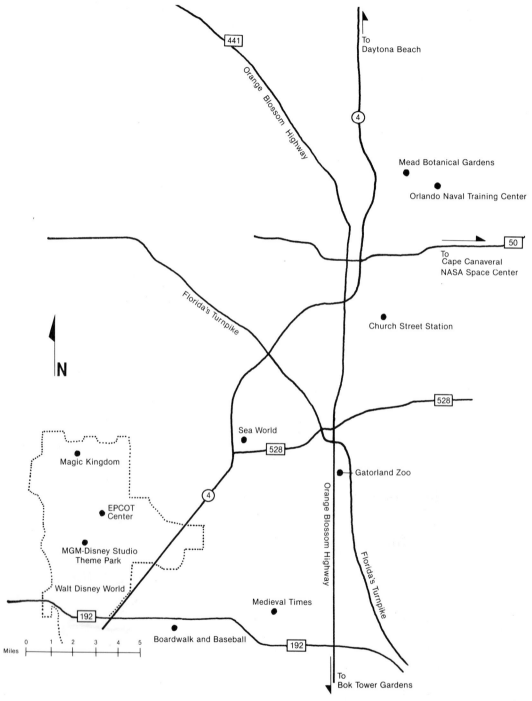

441

Orange Blossom Highway

To
Daytona Beach

4

Mead Botanical Gardens

Orlando Naval Training Center

50

To
Cape Canaveral
NASA Space Center

Florida's Turnpike

Church Street Station

N

528

Sea World

528

4

Magic Kingdom

EPCOT
Center

Gatorland Zoo

Orange Blossom Highway

Florida's Turnpike

MGM-Disney Studio
Theme Park

Walt Disney World

192

Miles 0 1 2 3 4 5

Medieval Times

Boardwalk and Baseball

192

To
Bok Tower Gardens

Orlando, Florida

Index
of People & Places